HOW TO DRAW AND PAINT

THE
OUTDOORS

HOW TO DRAW AND PAINT

THE OUTDOORS

MOIRA BUTTERFIELD

CHARTWELL
BOOKS, INC.

A QUARTO BOOK

Published by
Chartwell Books
A Division of Book Sales, Inc.
114 Northfield Avenue
Edison, New Jersey 08837

This edition produced for sale in the U.S.A. it's territories and dependencies only

Copyright © 1994 Quarto Publishing plc

ISBN 1-55521-912-8

This book was designed and produced by Quarto Children's Books Ltd,
The Fitzpatrick Building, 188-194 York Way, London N7 9QP

Art Director Louise Jervis
Series designer Nigel Bradley

Editor Jane Havell
Picture research Dipika Palmar-Jenkins, Sarah Risley

The publishers would like to thank Dawn Apperley for her artistic input.
Other illustrations by David Anstey and Guy Smith

Quarto would like to thank the following for providing photographs, and for granting permission to reproduce copyright material:

(a = *above*, b = *below*, c = *centre*, l = *left*, r = *right*)
Australian Tourist Commission: p82cr. Berry Bingel/*Ace:* p77bl.
Bridgeman Art Library: p61bl. Bridgeman Art Library/Giruadon: p20tr, p70 bl. Christies Images: p31al, p40bl.
Edmund Nagele/Ace: p30ar. Elizabeth Harden: p68ar. Ellie Gallwey: p20bl. E.T. Archive: p83al.
Mautitius/*Ace:* p72tr, p77al Mick Sharp: p82ar. *Mussee* D'Orsay: p33bl.
Paul Powis: p18cl. Rafael Marcia/Ace: p77br.

While every effort has been made to trace and acknowledge all copyright holders,
we would like to apologise should any omissions have been made.

Typeset In House
Manufactured by Bright Arts (Pte) Ltd, Singapore
Printed in Singapore by Star Standard Industries (Pte) Ltd, Singapore

Contents

Paints, pencils, and pots...

HERE WE SHOW YOU some of the most useful kinds of paints, crayons, pencils, and brushes. It is nice to build up a big collection if you're going to paint seriously, but you only need a few paints and some good brushes to make a start!

POWDER AND POSTER PAINTS

Powder paint comes in pots or in blocks. When you want to use it, you mix a little of the powder with water. Poster paint can come in jars or plastic bottles. You can use it straight from the container if you want it really thick, or thin it down with water.

WATERCOLORS

Watercolor paint is sold in blocks, which are easy to find and not expensive. Or it comes in tubes as "gouache," which is more professional and therefore a bit more expensive. You don't need a huge range, because you make different colors by mixing.

Watercolor blocks in a palette

Powder paint

Poster paint

Watercolor tubes

BRUSHES

You need a range of brushes for different techniques and effects - at least a fine pointed one, a middle thickness one, and a really thick one. Nylon is best for thinner paint, as it's soft; choose stiffer ones made of hog's hair for thick paint. You can also recycle household brushes for interesting effects. Try old toothbrushes and nailbrushes for spattering, and decorating brushes for big murals.

PENCILS, CRAYONS, AND PASTELS

Colored pencils are cheap to buy and come in a big range. For drawing, buy soft lead pencils, marked with B. A soft lead is much easier to rub out and won't leave a ridge in the paper if you don't press too hard. Also try wax crayons, chalks, pastels, and charcoal.

Pastels

Wax crayons

Soft lead pencils

Fibre-tip pens

Colored pencils

Clean water for mixing

Palette

PALETTES AND POTS

You can buy palettes for mixing colors, but an old plate or tray, or a piece of smooth wood, will do just as well.

Keeping notes

Y OU'LL WANT TO COLLECT ALL kinds of information to help you with your painting. Get into the habit of carrying a small sketchpad around so that you can jot down ideas and make quick sketches. Collect sketchpads made of different kinds of paper, and you'll have everything you need for painting with different techniques. You can then make a special "portfolio" of your best sketches and paintings.

COLLECTING INFORMATION

You can't always carry painting equipment with you, but you can put a notebook in your pocket! Look out for light effects, colors, and textures. Make quick sketches of scenes you like, so that you can work them up into paintings later. And collect small things you can paste in your notebook – leaves with nice colors, textures or shapes, for example.

PAPER TYPES

Paper is sold in different sizes, colors, thicknesses, and surfaces. You can buy it in sketchpads and in separate sheets. Cartridge paper is smooth, and is good for drawing and painting. Sugar paper is soft and slightly rough. It comes in lots of different colors and is great for pastels, crayons, and charcoal. Watercolor paper is extra thick so it doesn't wrinkle when wet paint is put on it. Start by buying two pads that are recommended for both painting and drawing, one white and one colored.

CREATING A PORTFOLIO

Your best drawings and paintings deserve a proper home, somewhere where they'll be safe from damage until you're ready to show them to people. Artists keep their work in a big folder called a "portfolio." You can make your own quite cheaply.

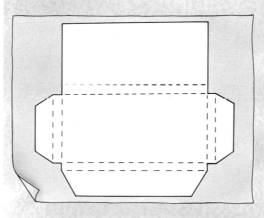

1 *Buy some big sheets of thick paper or thin card. Cut the corners out, as shown, to make flaps which will fold right over to make a big envelope. Fold the flaps in along the dotted lines.*

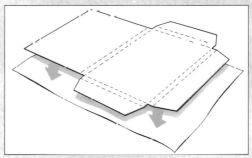

2 *Cut another sheet exactly to match the first, and glue them together. The double layer of paper will make the portfolio stronger.*

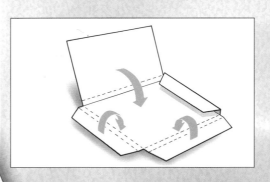

3 *Get some strong woven tape from a sewing shop, the sort that won't fray when you cut it. Glue a length firmly on to each side of the portfolio so that you can tie it shut.*

◄ *If you like, decorate the outside of the finished portfolio with paintings or prints. As your collection of work builds up, make more portfolios in different sizes and colors.*

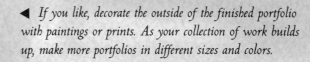

All shapes and sizes

IT IS A GOOD IDEA TO THINK ABOUT what you are going to draw before you start. Try drawing things roughly in pencil first to get the arrangement right. For instance, should that tree be in the middle of the paper, or at the side? The way in which a picture is organized is called its "composition." A well-composed picture will be interesting to look at.

PAPER SHAPES

Make sure that you choose the right size of paper for the picture you are going to paint, and also a piece the right shape. If you are going to paint a wide landscape, use a piece of paper that is wider than it is high. For something tall such as a building or a tree, use paper that is higher than it is wide.

◄

Try to avoid painting something very small with acres of blank space around it. Think about what you will put round the edges. If you don't want lots of things around a house, for instance, make the house itself bigger — or choose a smaller piece of paper.

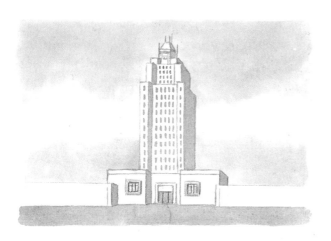

▲

This tall skyscraper looks a bit boring because it is right in the middle of a wide piece of paper. The walls on each side aren't very interesting, and they take attention away from the building. A higher, narrower piece of paper would be better.

▲

This is the right choice of paper size and shape. The picture goes right out to the edges, and there are interesting things over the whole area of the painting, not just in the middle where the trees are.

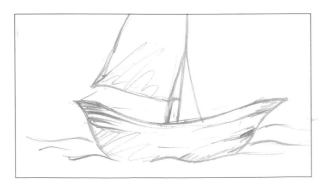

◄

The hull of this boat was drawn large to start with, and then there was not enough room to fit in the sail. If you rough out your drawing in pencil first, you won't make this kind of mistake.

14

THUMBS UP

Have you ever seen an artist stretching out an arm and sticking up a thumb? He is checking the size of something in the distance that he wants to paint.

The man's head comes to about halfway up the tree.

The tree looks twice as high as the artists's thumb.

I The artist is measuring a tree against his thumb. He finds that it is as high as two thumbs — one on top of the other.

2 He measures the size of a figure next to the tree. The person, being much closer, is as high as one thumb. Now he knows to draw the person half the height of the tree.

HOW TO MAKE A VIEWFINDER

WHAT YOU NEED
....

Card
Two paper clips
Ruler
Pencil
Scissors

You can use a viewfinder to help you decide which view to paint. This is a piece of card with a hole in the middle — our one is square, but you could make the hole any shape you like. Hold it in front of your chosen scene and you will see a mini-picture in the hole, just like looking through a camera.

I Cut a square or rectangle of card into two equal-sized L shapes - an old cereal box will do.

2 Clip the pieces together at the corners to make a square. Using the hand you don't draw with, hold the square in front of you. Rough out the picture inside the square quickly on your paper.

Mixing colors

MIXING COLORS IS ABOUT THE most important thing you'll ever do as a painter, so take time to read these pages and do lots of color experiments. Almost every color you can think of can be made using just three "primary" colors - red, yellow, and blue. Look at scenes in the sunlight and in shadow, and learn to see the different colors that you'll use on paper to recreate the view.

THE COLOR WHEEL

All nine colors in this wheel have been made from the three primary colors in the center. Practice making them with your paints. Start with yellow and add a bit of blue. See how your paint turns green! Mix any of the primary colors with the one next to it and you will get the one shown between them. Then, when you have made the colors on the inner circle, mix each of those with the ones next to them to get the colors on the outer circle.

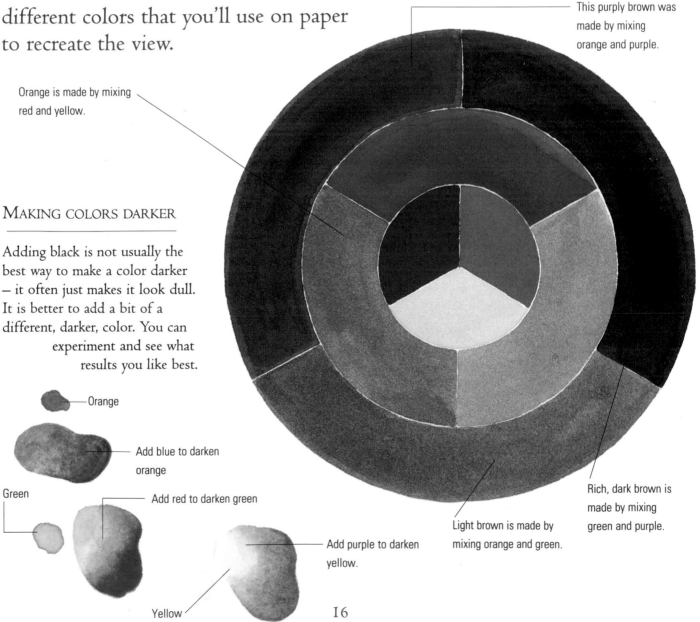

Orange is made by mixing red and yellow.

This purply brown was made by mixing orange and purple.

Light brown is made by mixing orange and green.

Rich, dark brown is made by mixing green and purple.

MAKING COLORS DARKER

Adding black is not usually the best way to make a color darker — it often just makes it look dull. It is better to add a bit of a different, darker, color. You can experiment and see what results you like best.

Orange

Add blue to darken orange

Green

Add red to darken green

Add purple to darken yellow.

Yellow

MAKING COLORS LIGHTER

Getting a lighter shade of color is done differently depending on what kind of paints or crayons you are using. With watercolor, make it thinner by adding more water. With poster paint, add some white, but only a little at a time. If you are using crayons, pastels, or wax crayons, just press more lightly.

Crayon

Poster paint

Watercolor

▲
You don't have to mix lots of colors to make a really good painting. This one was made with just two - blue and yellow - plus white. The two main colors mixed together made the green for the grass, while the white allowed lightening of each color for highlights. Restricting your palette in this way can make extremely effective pictures.

SEEING TONES IN COLOR

Look at the two pictures above. One is a color painting, and the other a black-and-white photograph of it. Looking at things without different colors is good practice for learning to see light and dark tones. See if you can paint a simple picture using just black and white, so that you can practice shadows and highlights.

Using colors

THE WAY YOU USE COLOR IN your paintings can have a big effect on their final look. Painting the same scene in "warm" colors and "cool" colors, for example, can completely transform the mood of a picture. Using "complementary" colors (see below) always makes a painting very vibrant and exciting. These rules are simple to learn and most artists find them worthwhile.

▲
Outdoor painters rarely use black to color shadows. They normally use shades of blue, sometimes mixed with the colors that they paint around the shadow. Blue shadows are especially right for snow scenes.

COMPLEMENTARY COLORS

The picture on the left was painted using very rich and deep colors that make the scene look very hot. The main colors in the composition are blue and orange. Now look back at the color wheel on page 16. Orange is the secondary color opposite the primary blue: the colors are called "complementary." Artists often use complementary colors for a strong composition.

▲
As well as the complementary blue and orange, there are greens and reds. The color wheel tells you that green is made from blue and yellow, so you can see how all the colors in this painting are very closely related to each other.

MAKING GRAYS AND BROWNS

Gray doesn't have to be made from black and white! These mixes show how you get interesting darker shades from combining primary and complementary colors.

The pictures on this page are all made using restricted color schemes. The primary colors are used with the secondaries made from them, or with their complementary colors. They have a range of feelings, but all are very dramatic and strong.

◄

All three primary colors - blue, yellow, and red - are used here. The blue and yellow, mixed, produce the orange. See how the shadows on the sand contain lots of yellow.

Red is the complementary color of green.

Green is made from blue and yellow.

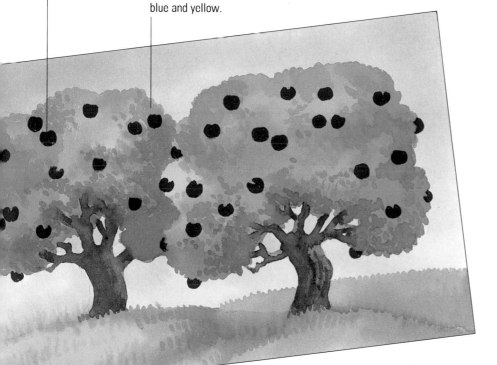

▲

This forest scene is a study of many different shades of gray and brown. They are made mostly using the greens and yellows in the same picture.

▲

The apple orchard is painted using the "cool" colors - blues and greens. They make the composition harmonious, but the spots of bright red, complementary to the green, brighten it up.

▲

This fire looks really hot! Paint one of your own using the "warm" colors of red, yellow, orange, and orangey brown.

Brush strokes

DIFFERENT BRUSHES CAN GIVE you very different effects. Experiment with them to see what you like, and to give you practice. Always choose the right kind and size of brush for different techniques. If you want to paint colors made up of dots, use a small round brush; for dashes, use a broader one.

Choose colors for each area that are close in tone, so that you build up a gradual effect.

PAINTING IN DOTS

For painting in lots of dots, choose fine round-headed brushes. "The Harbour at Bessin Port," by George Seurat, is very striking because of this technique. If you stand back, the colors look solid, but if you go close you can see that each tiny dot is quite separate.

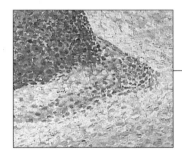

You can vary the length of the dashes, and even their direction.

PAINTING IN DASHES

For quite large dashes, use brushes which end in a square shape, called flats. The painting on the left, by Eli Gallwey, is made up of dashes of different colored paint.

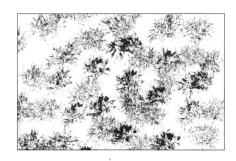

▲

Use dryish paint on a fine round brush, and let each color dry before you add more.

▲

Use a flat brush, again fairly dry, to make short sweeps across a ground color.

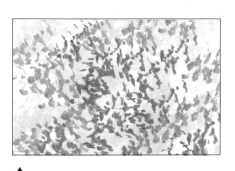

▲

Use a flat brush, lightly pressed on and lifted up immediately, with the ground still wet.

Apply the stippling on top of wet paint for a smudgy look.

PAINTING STIPPLES

Stippling is putting lots of tiny dots on top of another layer of paint. You do it with quite a stiff brush, either round or flat. For this jug of flowers, the blue of the jug was left to dry before the stippling was done. The flowers were stippled while still wet, to mix the colors up more.

Put the white stippling on after the blue has dried, so that it stays separate.

Look, no brushes!

YOU DON'T HAVE TO USE BRUSHES OR crayons to make paintings. You can put paint on to paper with all sorts of things – sponges, scraps of fabric, scrunched-up paper, card. Look round your home for old things you could use, particularly materials with an interesting texture which would come through on to the paper.

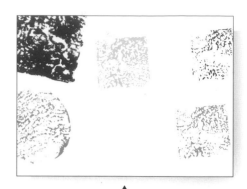

▲
This picture was made by dabbing paint on with different bits of packaging material.

DABBING AND SPONGING

Applying paint with a sponge is very easy, and a good way to cover large areas quickly and evenly. Don't let the sponge get too wet with paint, or the texture won't come through. You can also cut up old packaging material into different shapes and use them as little printing blocks.

Folded pad of bubble packaging.

Polystyrene packaging cut into shapes.

▲
Dip a sponge in thick paint and dab or drag it on to the paper. Experiment with different effects as the sponge gets dryer.

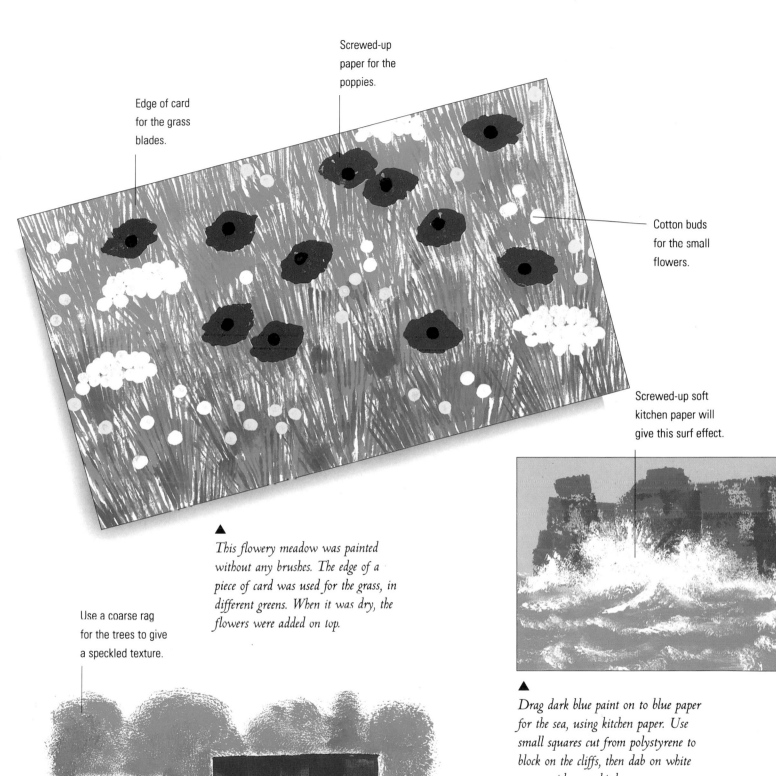

Screwed-up paper for the poppies.

Edge of card for the grass blades.

Cotton buds for the small flowers.

Screwed-up soft kitchen paper will give this surf effect.

▲

This flowery meadow was painted without any brushes. The edge of a piece of card was used for the grass, in different greens. When it was dry, the flowers were added on top.

Use a coarse rag for the trees to give a speckled texture.

▲

Drag dark blue paint on to blue paper for the sea, using kitchen paper. Use small squares cut from polystyrene to block on the cliffs, then dab on white spray with more kitchen paper.

◄

Drag on paint thickly for the grass, roofs, and walls using the side of a piece of stiff card. This gives even blocks of color. When the paint is dry, drag over them again in places with darker color using much less paint, to make shading. Cut a small piece of card to drag for the fence.

23

Using pastels

PASTELS ARE MADE SIMPLY OF pigment and gum, and are soft and crumbly. They make brightly colored lines and can also give a delicate, blurry effect if you rub over them with a rag or a fingertip. You can buy pastels made into sticks or pencils. Sticks easily pick up dirt so store them in a box carefully laid side by side.

You cannot easily mix pastels or put them on top of each other to make new colors. However, pastel sets usually have a wide range of shades to choose from.

Putty rubber for erasing pastel marks

Pastel sticks

PASTEL TIPS

Pastels look very good on colored paper. Many artists use grey paper to get a soft effect. Black paper makes the colors look really bright.

Use the broad edge of a dark brown stick for the cliff.

Use white strokes and dabs for the froth.

With the thin edge of the stick, use different greens in up-and-down strokes for the grass.

Autumn-style colors used together.

Watery-style colors used together.

▲

Get a blurred effect by rubbing your pastel marks with a clean dry rag. You can make exciting movement lines in this way. It's also good for doing skies and water.

PASTEL PROJECTS

This beautiful Christmas tree is easy to draw. Choosing black paper makes the colors of the shining fairy lights very bright.

1 Draw a trunk in brown. Put in some curved lines for branches, in different shades of green and blue.

2 Use a clean dry rag or sponge to rub over the lines you have made. Rub gently in the same direction as the branches. Then add splodges of bright color for the lights.

3 Rub gently over the lights, using a circular movement, to give them a soft glow.

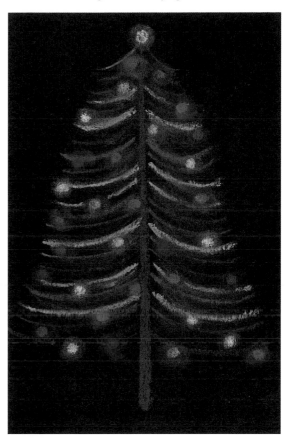

Broad, wavy strokes of blue and white suggest the sea.

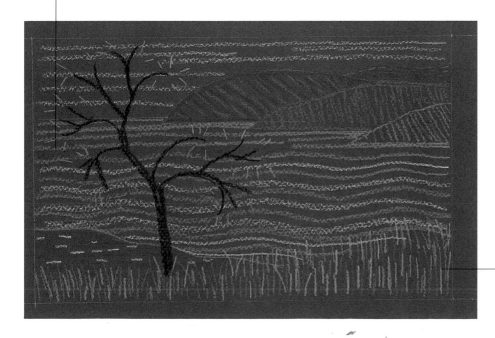

◄

You can make a lively picture, full of movement, by using small strokes of pastel, with no rubbing or shading. Make your strokes follow the shapes you want to show. For instance, grass is best with strokes that go up and down. Sea is made with wavy strokes going across the page. Use both the thin and broad edges of the pastel to vary the effects.

Up-and-down strokes for the grass look good in different greens.

Charcoal and chalk

CHARCOAL AND CHALK ARE GREAT FOR doing quick sketches that have sweeping lines and wide areas of light and shade. Both are soft and powdery and can be used to give a textured effect.

Charcoal, made from burnt wood, is very dark gray, black if you use it heavily. You can smudge it with your finger, which makes very good shading. It comes in different thicknesses.

Chalk and chalk pastels are pale and come in many colors. They can look very effective if used on a dark-colored paper, or with charcoal.

CHOOSING PAPER

If you use charcoal or chalk with rough paper, the pattern of the paper's surface will show through. This will give your picture an interesting texture.

TEXTURES

These are just some of the different texture and line effects that you can get with chalk. Try them out yourself.

Dabs and dots can be softened by smudging with a finger.

Shapes can be drawn into chalk using an eraser with a fine edge.

Crosshatching

Wide areas can be drawn with the broad side of a chalk stick.

26

Smudge the charcoal with your fingertips to create a smoky effect.

Use the broad edge of a charcoal stick to make a thick stroke.

Press lightly and the grain of the paper will show.

SMOKY STEAM TRAIN

This charcoal drawing of a train has been drawn using a number of techniques. The edges of each part have been drawn with firm strokes of the fine edge. Shading is done using the broad edge, lightly for the gray, and more heavily for the front of the engine. Look how the streaks and smoke puffs by the wheels give a feeling of speed.

USING CHARCOAL AND CHALK

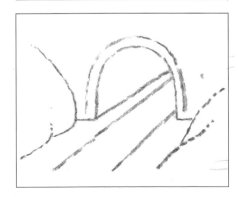

1 Sketch in the main lines of your picture lightly with the thin edge of the charcoal — the tunnel, the rail track, and the bank.

2 Smudge in the dark shadow in the tunnel. Start to add outline detail to the grass and the bricks.

3 Using colored chalks, give the bricks a range of colors and make the ground beneath the tracks look rough and stony.

Putting it in perspective

WHEN YOU LOOK AT A LANDSCAPE you will see that it stretches away into the distance. Some things look larger because they are nearer, other things look small because they are further away. It can be quite difficult to create this effect on paper. Getting all the parts of your picture the right size in relation to each other, and in the right place so that they look as if they disappear into the distance, is called putting them in perspective.

PARALLEL LINES

Parallel lines look as if they are joining together as they stretch into the distance. This is an important part of perspective. The further away your vanishing point is, the longer they will take to join.

▲

This photograph would make a good composition for a painting. The furrows of the plowed field, apparently getting narrower as they stretch away, draw the eye into the distance. The contrast between the light and shade on the furrows increases the effect and is very dramatic.

HOW TO DRAW A ROAD

A road makes a good subject for practicing perspective drawing. In reality, everyone knows a road stays about the same width, so the vanishing point in your picture shows very clearly. Here we show you the effect of putting the vanishing point in two different places — in the center and to one side. See which effect you like best.

1 *First start with your horizon line, and put in a pale wash of green and blue for the land and the sky.*

2 *Mark the vanishing point lightly in pencil on the horizon. Here it is in the center.*

3 *Draw lines down from the vanishing point as guides for the road, the sidewalk, and the fence.*

4 *Here is the same picture, with a vanishing point more to the left. See how the trees on the left now line up.*

AN OUTSIDE VANISHING POINT

You can make a vanishing point outside the edge of your picture. To help you, mark it on another piece of paper next to the one you are going to paint on.

PLOWED FIELDS

Draw lines coming out of a vanishing point off the page above the horizon line. Use these to guide you to draw plow furrows coming down from the vanishing point. Draw some lines across, too, to show the divisions of the fields. A tractor and a farmhouse, small because they are away in the distance, complete your picture.

Seeing into the distance

Here are some of the ways to make your pictures look as if they are stretching into the distance. Put objects in perspective and use vanishing points (see pages 28-29). Overlap things, so that one object looks as if it is behind another. Make things big at the front of your picture and smaller at the back. Remember that the further away things are, the less clear their outline.

▲

Green hills change with distance to look quite blue. Colors also get paler as things get further away. Make your colors at the front stronger than they are at the back.

▲

Try a picture of a landscape seen from indoors through a window. First paint the window round the edge.

◄

Landscape painters rarely use black to color shadows. They normally use shades of blue mixed with the colors that they paint around the shadow. First check which way the shadows lie.

In the foreground, edges are distinct and colors separate, as in the bench in the picture on the left. Further away, in the distant fields, edges get fuzzier and colors tend to look mixed together - the church tower is just a light splodge of brown.

◀

Constable's "A Park Glade" is a view of Dedham Church - but you can only just see it!

BLUE HORIZON

If you look at a range of grassy hills you will see that the green color tends to turn soft blue the further away it is. Try a picture like the one below. Overlap the hills as they slope towards the water. Start off with strong greens and distinct blades of grass at the front. Add blue and white to the greens as you paint to the back.

The palest color should be at the back.

A mid-tone would be right here.

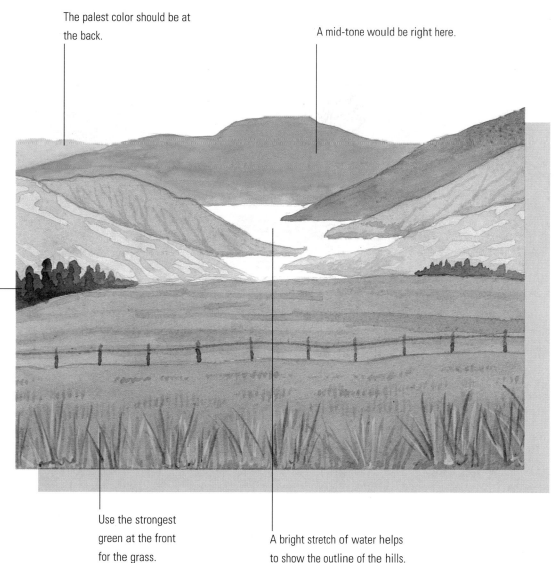

Dark green trees help define the slope of the field.

Use the strongest green at the front for the grass.

A bright stretch of water helps to show the outline of the hills.

Looking at light

The sun's light has a very important effect on outside scenes and colors. For most of the day the sun is not directly overhead, but shines on things at an angle. The area behind an object is blocked from the light and in shadow. You need to note where the sun is and what directions the shadows fall in. Weather has an effect, too. On an overcast day, not only are there no clear shadows, but the light is softer and more even.

▲

Here are some of the different green colors used to paint this tree. Look how different the greens are on the sunny and the shady sides.

LIGHT AND COLOR

Look at the leaves on a tree. You will see that they are made up of several different greens — some light and some dark. Up close, with the light even, they are mostly the same color, but when light shines on them at different angles from a distance they look different.

▲

The sand on a beach looks all the same color on a dull day, but in strong sunlight shadows make lots of variations.

▲

When the sun is low in the sky, shadows are much more pronounced. The hollows between the dunes look almost black.

Painting by the Clock

The same scene looks very different from one hour to the next as the light changes. You can use this effect to make an unusual picture.

Make a preliminary sketch of an outdoor scene. Paint the scene at four different times of the day, carefully noting how the colors change. At early morning and evening, for example, when the sun is low in the sky, the light is more red. Cut your paintings into four quarters. Fit one quarter from each scene together to make a new picture.

Sunrise

Sunset

Morning

Afternoon

The Impressionists

The Impressionists were a group of painters in the late nineteenth century, famous for their studies of the effects of light on color. Look out for their work in galleries and art books.

Claude Monet painted this picture called "Haystacks." He did not use strong outlines but created all the shapes using different colors. Look at the picture from about ten feet away, and the grass and haystacks seem to be solid colors. In fact they are made up of an amazing number of different colors, all created by the effects of light.

Painting shadows

W**HEN LIGHT SHINES ON AN** object, the object casts a shadow on the ground. If you put shadows into a picture, it helps to make it look more real and gives it a 3D feel. Look carefully at the scene you are painting to work out where the shadows fall. Roughly sketch them when you are planning your picture at the beginning.

See how the side of the block is darker than the top.

The back is the darkest because it gets no light.

WHAT IS A SHADOW?

Quite simply, a shadow is the area behind an object that is blocked from the light. It therefore appears as a dark area the same shape as the object.

CHANGING SHADOWS

As the sun moves across the sky, the shadows of a stationary object move, too. Try this painting experiment to see for yourself. Do it on a sunny day, when the shadows are clear and sharp. Put your card figure outside if you can. Indoors, use a table in front of a big window where the sun shines in for most of the day. Sketch the figure and the shape of the shadows at different times.

2 *Stand your figure facing south. In the morning, the sun is in the east, and casts a shadow to the right.*

3 *At noon, the sun is directly overhead, and slightly to the south. The shadow is very short.*

1 *Cut out a simple person shape from a piece of card. Leave extra card at the bottom. Turn this back to make a stand.*

4 *By the afternoon, the sun has moved round to the west, and the shadow is cast to the left of the figure.*

5 *Late in the evening, the shadow is very long and stretched out. This can make very dramatic effects in outdoor painting.*

How many shadows?

When only one light is shining, such as the sun, an object will cast only one shadow. If more than one light is shining, shadows become more complicated!

Go outside or look out of a window one evening when there are several street lights or window lights on. There will be lots of different shadows going different ways. Try sketching them quickly and use your sketches to make an interesting painting later on.

Shadow Shapes

◀

Compare the shape of the tree and the shape of the shadow. To make your pictures real, details like this are very important.

The snowman has two shadows because he is standing between two lights.

Look at the way the shadows fall on the sidewalk

▲

Look at the shape of the railings, and see how their shadows have the same shape, but slightly distorted because of the angle from which the light is shining.

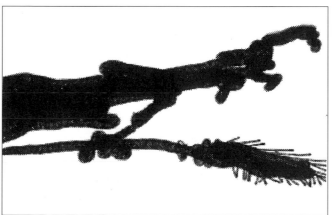

Scary shadows

Shadows sometimes look frightening because they can make mysterious, distorted shapes, especially in the evening when the low sun makes them stretch out longer. You can use this effect to paint a sinister, dramatic picture with mystery shadows that suggest scary monsters!

Using shading

IF YOU LOOK AT AN OBJECT YOU WILL
see that some parts of it look dark and
some parts look light. This is called tone.
It is caused by the way that light falls –
the brightest parts are where the light is
shining directly on to the object. You add
tone by shading the parts of the object
that are away from the direct light source.
This makes things look very solid.

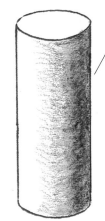

USING TONE OUTSIDE

Look carefully at the things you
are going to paint or draw. The
parts that face away from the sun
will have a darker tone than the
parts facing the light.

This side of
the house is in
shadow.

▲

*This house has been shaded so that one side is darker than
the other. It makes clear from which direction the sun is
coming, so the house looks realistic.*

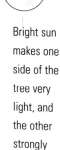

Bright sun
makes one
side of the
tree very
light, and
the other
strongly
shaded.

When the
sun is not
bright, the
differences
between
light and
shade are
much less
marked.

MODELLING OBJECTS

When you are shading an object, the
marks you make should follow its shape.
To make something look round, use
rounded strokes of your brush.

Without shadows,
the cube would
not look solid.

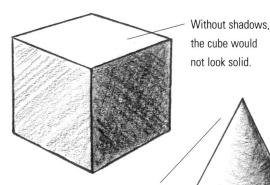

To make a cone shape,
use shading down one
edge, fading away
towards the center.

The shading down
one edge of the
cylinder fades away
as it rounds the curve.

This is the hardest
shape to do. Shading
fades way towards
the center to make a
crescent shape.

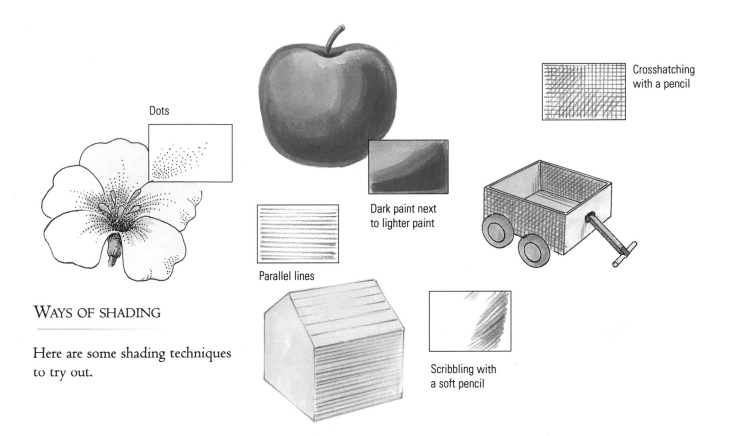

Dots

Crosshatching
with a pencil

Dark paint next
to lighter paint

Parallel lines

WAYS OF SHADING

Here are some shading techniques
to try out.

Scribbling with
a soft pencil

BY MOONLIGHT

Moonlight creates tone
and shadows in the
same way as sunlight.
Try doing a moonlight
picture on dark paper.
First work out where
the moon is shining
from. Then add
shading, shadows and
highlights in the same
way as for a sunny
picture.

A landscape in layers

HERE IS AN EASY WAY TO MAKE AN OUTDOOR painting really look as if it is 3D! It is made up of layers, one behind the other, so the distances really look convincing. Look again at the pages on perspective and distance painting for tips. Always make the foreground stronger and more detailed than the faraway parts.

WHAT YOU NEED

Thin bendy card

Crayons or paints

Pencil

Scissors

Glue

Ruler

PUTTING IT ALL TOGETHER

Making this layered painting is almost like constructing a little toy theater! When you have made the back, sides, and front frame (steps 1 to 4 on the left), you'll be left with four rectangles of card. These are used for your painting.

1 *Cut out six rectangles of card each measuring 9 x 7 inches. Cut out two square pieces each measuring 7 x 7 inches.*

2 *Paint one of the rectangles of card blue for the sky. Cut another rectangle into a frame shape, by cutting out an even hole 8 x 6 inches, which leaves a half-inch frame all the way round. Decorate the frame with your paints any way you like.*

3 *Use the two square pieces for the sides. Mark them in pencil in seven inch-wide sections. Draw straight lines with a ruler to indicate the sections, and get an adult to score down each line with a sharp knife. Then fold them along the scored lines to make concertina shapes*

4 *Glue the side pieces to the front of the sky piece – the sky piece forms the back. Then glue the frame to the front.*

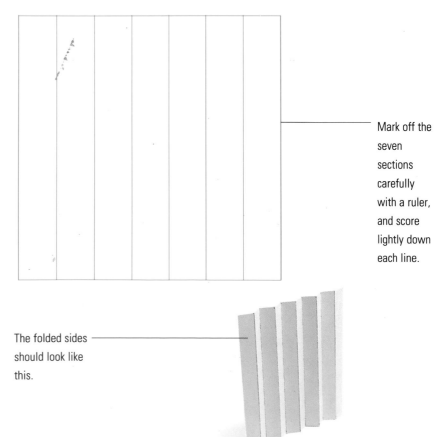

Mark off the seven sections carefully with a ruler, and score lightly down each line.

The folded sides should look like this.

PAINTING THE PICTURE

Use your four rectangles of card to make the picture. First sketch the picture on a single piece of paper for reference. Then decide how to divide it up. Cut out along the top outline of each piece.

▼

When you have finished each piece, put a little glue down the sides of each card. Slot them, in the right order, into the sides of the frame. Push them right down to the bottom and leave them to dry.

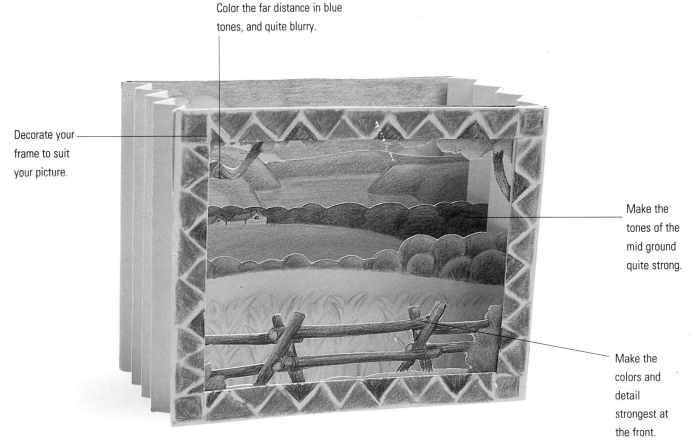

Color the far distance in blue tones, and quite blurry.

Decorate your frame to suit your picture.

Make the tones of the mid ground quite strong.

Make the colors and detail strongest at the front.

Make it flat!

Y OU DON'T HAVE TO USE PERSPECTIVE IN a picture or try to make it look realistic if you don't want to. You can paint what you see in your own way. Many painters are more interested in using flat patterns, bright colors, and interesting shapes than in making their paintings look "real." This is called "abstract" painting. When you are painting realistically, you need to keep objects in the right scale. But in abstract paintings, scale does not matter so much. In the picture on the right the leaf, the window of the house and the pond are all the same size!

◄

The artist Paul Klee called this picture "Sea Ghost." You can see two fish, some blue wiggly lines for the water, and brown and green in the background. He didn't use perspective, and he didn't try to make his picture look real. The fun is in working out what is there, and what you think it all means.

Here is a landscape with lots of things you would see outside. There are two different kinds of leaves, a blue sky with clouds, parts of a house, and a garden with a pond and a fence. They don't look realistic, though, because there is no perspective, no scale, and the shapes are arranged to make nice patterns on the page. You could do the same!

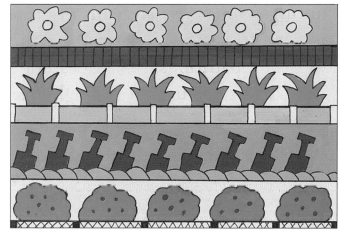

This scene looks more real than the top one, because it has scale, perspective, and a convincing arrangement. But the shapes are still abstract. Try the idea yourself, using the shapes shown here.

This picture started with soft pencil lines drawn across the page with a ruler. Between the lines, the artist painted rows of things you might see in a garden. Then he made the ruled lines into different kinds of fences.

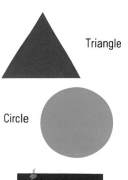

Triangle

Circle

Rectangle

Rhomboid (a rectangle leaning over to one side)

41

Printing pictures

PATTERNS AND SHAPES LOOK really interesting if you print them. Printing is using an object to transfer the paint to the paper. It is the best method for building up a picture from lots of repeat patterns. If the printing "block" has a texture on it, this will come through, too.

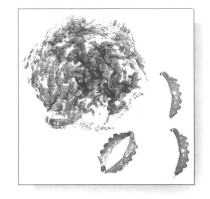

Celery stick

POTATO PRINTING

Potato halves make brilliant printing blocks, and are easy to get hold of. Cutting them out can be quite tricky to start with, so practice with simple shapes, such as the star shown here. Cut a large potato in half cleanly. Let it dry a bit. Then draw your shape on to the cut half with a fine felt-tip pen. With a sharp knife, cut round the outline. Cut the surrounding edges away so that the shape stands out by at least a quarter-inch.

WHAT YOU NEED

....

Poster paint

An old tray

Sponge

Knife

Old rags

Cabbage leaves

1 *Put some paint on to a flat sponge so that it soaks in well. This is your printing pad. If you can, prepare several with different colors.*

2 *Press the potato block firmly and evenly into the printing pad.*

3 *Press the inked block firmly on to your paper for a second or two, then lift it off cleanly. You'll be able to make several prints before you need to re-ink your block.*

▲ *Mushroom halves make a very attractive shape, with their curved tops and straight stems. Try printing them in different colors.*

MAKING THE MOST OF VEGETABLES

Lots of other vegetables make good printing blocks. Look for ones with interesting textures. Here we are using cabbage leaves, whole celery sticks, pepper rings, thin celery slices, mushroom halves, and halved cauliflower florets. You can either press them into an inked sponge pad, or paint on them with a thick brush. Then print them on paper in the same way as the potato block.

Cabbage leaves

Think thick!

USE EXTRA THICK PAINT TO GIVE YOUR pictures a more interesting surface. Mix powder paints thickly by adding only a little water. If you use paints from a bottle or tube, don't add any water at all – or, instead of water, mix tube paint with fine sand. Try spreading paint on with a palette knife or a plastic picnic knife instead of using a brush.

Always put thick paint on to thick paper or card. Thin paper will tear very easily.

HOW TO MAKE POSTER PAINT EXTRA THICK

• mix it with washing-up liquid and a few drops of water.
• mix it with fine sand, but don't make it too thick to spread over the paper.
• leave your sand overnight to dry. When it is dry, dust off the loose grains.
• mix it with flour and water.

Scrape lines with the edge of your knife.

Dab on leaves for the tree.

▼
The grainy texture of this sand painting makes the shells look particularly realistic. Instead of mixing paint with sand, you could use thick poster paint on sandpaper for a similar effect.

▲
Look at the sky and grass in this farmyard scene. These large areas of thick colors have been put on with a palette knife. If you don't have one, a plastic picnic knife will do just as well.

This sea scene was created using acrylic paints, which dry very quickly. The boat's sails have been painted in white and gray. Different shades of blue and green are used to make the sea look textured. It is easy to give the water a feeling of movement by adding touches of white paint to the tops of the waves. Notice how the small dabs of red stand out clearly from the rest of the scene.

Splash on white over the blue paint.

Never use a pure black for shadows, but mix it with a little blue.

By using your palette or plastic knife in bold sweeps you can create imaginative land or seascapes.

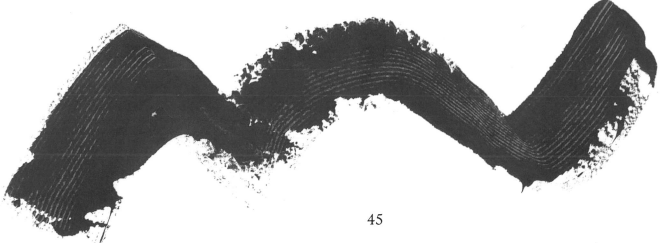

Dragging and combing

YOU CAN MAKE EVEN lines and patterns in thick paint by dragging things through it. This is a good technique for making waves, waterfalls or patterns in the sky.

WAVES AND STRIPES

These are some of the simple shapes that you can create by dragging a comb through wet, thick paint.

A medium comb used straight.

A medium comb used in a curve.

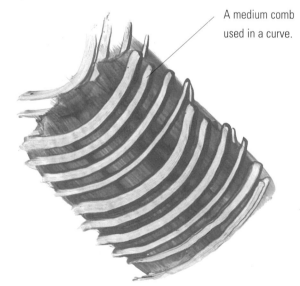

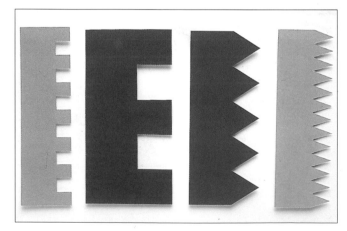

Cut out different comb shapes from a piece of stiff card or from some old plastic packaging.

Circles made
with the end of
a paintbrush.

As well as different-shaped combs, you can
drag other things through paint. Try using
the ends of pencils and paintbrushes, of
different widths. For a very fine effect, you
could use paper-clips or nails.

MAKING YOUR MARK

To make the sea scene below, start
with dragging the background
areas of yellow and blue. Keep the
paint thick. This will give you
continuous swirly lines right
across the page. Then make the
fish, using a range of comb
shapes, cut them out and stick
them on the sea. We have also
made starfish, a shell, and some
seaweed to put on the beach.

Waxing and scratching

Wax crayons are waterproof. If you paint over them with watery paint they show through because the paint runs off the wax. You can cover wax if the paint is thick enough - use poster paint for this. Then you can scratch through it to show the wax colors beneath. This is ideal for making night pictures or the flickering flames of fires.

▲

Broad diagonal lines of yellow and red wax are good for a fire scene. Cover them with thick black paint and then scratch through to make tongue shapes of fire.

SCRATCHING WAX

Cover the paper with thick lines of wax crayon — use one color or lots of different ones as you like. Then paint thickly over the whole sheet with poster paint. You may need two coats.

▲

Here, yellow, orange, and red wax was put on first, then thickly covered with dark blue poster paint for a night scene. When the paint is dry, scratch lines through it with the end of your paintbrush.

▶

Use lots of different colored wax crayons beneath dark blue or black paint to make a dazzling firework explosion.

▲

To make this flying night owl, cover the paper with white wax. Paint thick black on top, then scratch out the owl shape. You can then color in the owl with more wax crayons.

USING WATERY PAINT

If you use watery poster paints, or thin watercolors, on top of the wax, they will run off the wax without needing to be scratched out. This is a very good technique for making clear white outlines or white shading – for example, ripples on water or light clouds in the sky. Don't make the top coat too watery, though, or the paper will crinkle.

2 *Using thin poster paint or watercolor, start painting in your colors. You'll see all the white outlines showing through.*

1 *First draw a light pencil outline of your picture. Draw white wax lines over all your pencil*

▼

Here, the white wax outlines are very good for making clouds in the sky and froth on the edge of the sea.

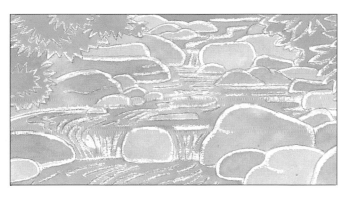

3 *Finish with strong greens for the trees, and darken some of the gray stones to add variation. The white outlines look like sunlight on the water and the wet stones.*

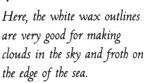

Watercolors

WATERCOLOR PAINTS MAKE DELICATE colors that are good for landscapes. You can buy them in tubes or blocks and they are easy to carry around outdoors for making quick color sketches. However, watercolor technique is known to be quite tricky. For one thing, you can't have second thoughts, because there isn't a satisfactory way to correct mistakes once the paint is dry. You should certainly practice indoors first! It's a good idea to start by using photographs – either copy them exactly, or use them to give you ideas.

Always use watercolors with clean water. If you use dirty water you will make a muddy mess! Set up two jars – one for mixing paint and one for cleaning brushes. If you can, borrow some paints first to experiment. If you decide you like using them, you can buy them later.

STRETCHING PAPER

You can buy white watercolor paper in separate sheets or in pads. It comes in lots of different thicknesses and surfaces. The easist thing is to buy special thick paper that won't crinkle when you put the wet paint on it. If you use thinner, or professional, watercolor paper you will need to stretch it before you use it.

You stretch watercolor paper by wetting it and leaving it to dry while it is taped to a board. You must let it dry slowly, and not in sunshine or by a fire.

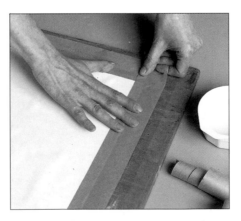

1 Soak a sheet of paper in water for about ten minutes. Then lift it out carefully and lay it on a flat, clean board. Tape the edges of the paper to the board with brown tape called gumstrip. You need to wet the back of the gumstrip to make it sticky.

2 When the paper is completely dry, you can lay on a background wash of a pale color. Leaving the paper taped down, put on the color in broad sweeps with a wide, soft brush. When this background color is dry, you can start painting details.

A WATERCOLOR SKETCH

Artists tend to use watercolor to make a dreamy impression of a scene, rather than a very realistic, detailed picture. Before you start, choose the colors you want to use and lay them within reach.

If you do make a mistake, you can often manage to remove paint while it is still wet by pressing the area gently with a soft, damp sponge. Many famous artists in the past used bread for this trick!

1 Use a thick brush and broad strokes to lay down a pale wash for the sky and another pale wash for the land.

2 While the washes are still wet, add some darker paint to make blurry trees and mountains.

3 When the paint for the groundwork is dry, add details with a fine brush. Once watercolor is dry, you can work on top of it with pastels or chalks for different effects and greater detail.

51

Watery paint

YOU CAN GET SOME WONDERFUL effects if you put wet paint on to wet paper. The paint dries to give a very even, soft result, which makes good skies and seas. You can use watercolors or watered-down poster paint, but you must stretch the paper first. Otherwise it will go crinkly when it dries.

WORKING WITH TWO COLORS

First wet the paper by painting clean water evenly all over it with a wide, soft brush. Apply a single color and you will get an even wash. Depending on the effect you want, either wait for it to dry, or apply the next color immediately. You need to work pretty quickly!

Put on the second color without too much water on the brush, and brush gently over the wet edges.

Paint in clouds with poster or acrylic paint.

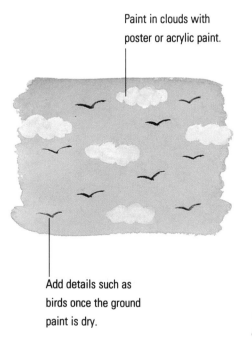

Add details such as birds once the ground paint is dry.

Load a thick brush with the second color and drip it on to the wet ground paint. For a runny effect, tilt the paper slightly.

A GLOWING SUNSET

The warm colors of a sunset sky make a good subject for painting wet on wet. First have all the colors you will want to use for the background ready to hand. Prepare the paper by painting clean water all over it with a wide, soft brush.

I *With the paper still wet, apply an even wash of yellow with a wide brush. Then add broad strokes of orangey red.*

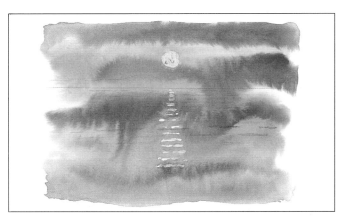

2 *With a clean brush, put in dark blue for the sky, and pale blue for the sea in the foreground. The edges will run together.*

3 *Leave the groundwork colors to dry. Then add details, such as the fishing boats with their reflections, the sun, and blue strokes over the golden water.*

Drawing buildings

Y OU CAN DRAW BUILDINGS THAT LOOK flat or you can give them depth by using perspective. Look at pages 28-29 for tips on perspective drawing and practice with the exercise here if you aren't too sure. Plan your picture first. Sketch it in lightly before you start to draw or paint it properly.

A BASIC HOUSE SHAPE

Try this perspective exercise. Once you have done it a few times, use the same ideas to make different-shaped houses.

3 *Add a roof and windows at the side. Remember that the shaded side will be darker than the others.*

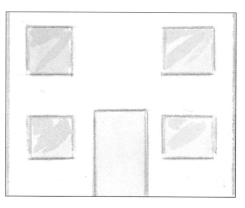

1 *Start by using a ruler to draw the house front. Using watercolor, light chalks or pastels, color it a pale stone color. Add a door and windows.*

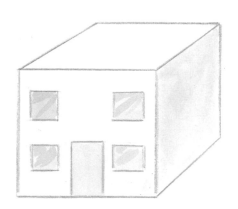

2 *Draw in the sides to make a cube. Use lines drawn lightly to a vanishing point if this helps you. You can rub them out afterwards.*

▲

You can get very good effects by contrasting the angular shapes of buildings with the soft shapes of the natural landscape. Here, the squareness of the house makes a good point of focus among the rounded trees and curved path.

▲

You can still give a sense of perspective even if you paint a square building from the front so that the sides don't show. Here, the shadows cast by the overhanging roof, and the shading on the fence and the grass, all help to create a feeling of distance.

COMPLICATED SHAPES

If you want to draw a complicated building, it's best to sketch it out first using simple shapes. Try to see what the main shapes are - circles, rectangles, etc. When you've got the basic outline, it's much easier to fill in the details.

4 *Add details to the walls, roof and windows. For extra realism, have the house cast a shadow on one side.*

▶

Here is a dramatic building shape for you to copy. Sketch it out first using basic shapes. Look how the skyscraper gets narrower at the top, which increases the sense of perspective and makes it look very tall.

55

Cityscapes

CITY SCENES ARE FULL OF exciting shapes and patterns. They are ideal for making busy pictures with lots of different textures and brushmarks. Don't be put off thinking they look too difficult – the trick is to look at everything carefully, and see the patterns and shapes in the buildings.

▲

In this picture, the triangular shapes of the distant factory roofs and the tall straight telegraph poles dominate the composition. See what other shapes you can find.

BASIC SHAPES

In the city there are lots of shapes made up of straight lines. Make a simplified city picture using the shapes you see. Color them with bright strong colors using wax, pastels, or poster paint, or a mixture of all three! Make sure you look closely at the buildings first, and include any distinguishing features, such as odd-shaped windows, towers, and clocks.

▲

This picture makes the city view look flat, although there is perspective and a sense of depth caused by buildings being behind each other. The bright colors make it a lot of fun.

BRICKWORK

There are several ways of painting brickwork on a building. If you are doing a close-up, you need to show the pattern in detail.

1 *Wash over the wall area with flat color. Wait for it to dry.*

2 *Put dabs of a different color on top.*

3 *Paint lines around the dabs with pale color to show the mortar.*

Use a fine black biro or drawing pen to mark in the outlines and details of the buildings.

PEN AND WASH

This method combines drawing and painting. A fine pen means you can add lots of detail.

Paint soft watery washes over the buildings, sky, and foreground.

MAKING A PRINT

If you look down from a high building you'll see many different roof shapes. They are ideal for making a print of a city picture.

WHAT YOU NEED

Thick card
Block of wood or polystyrene
Poster paint
Old plate or tray
Glue
Rags
Paper

1 *Cut out a simple roof shape from thick card. Spread glue over the block and press the card down on it.*

2 *When the glue is dry press the card down into paint mixed in a plate or a tray.*

3 *Press the card down several times on the paper. Wipe it with a damp rag before changing colors. Draw details with a pen*

Industrial scenes

ONCE YOU HAVE PRACTICED DRAWING AND painting buildings separately, you can start putting them all together in different kinds of views. Don't just think about people's houses and apartments. Town centers full of shops make good subjects, and so do industrial scenes, such as factories, warehouses, and power stations. These often have very dramatic outlines, and interesting machinery to paint. You can experiment with different lighting - try painting a factory at night under floodlights!

▲
Sketch out the outline of two or three skylines. Paint alternate ones in black, one behind the other, to give the effect of a big city.

◄
Factories, power stations, building sites, and docks make exciting outdoor pictures. Use charcoal and chalk smudged with your finger to make a smoky scene.

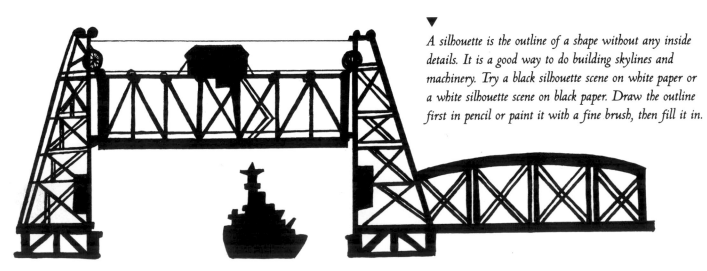

▼
A silhouette is the outline of a shape without any inside details. It is a good way to do building skylines and machinery. Try a black silhouette scene on white paper or a white silhouette scene on black paper. Draw the outline first in pencil or paint it with a fine brush, then fill it in.

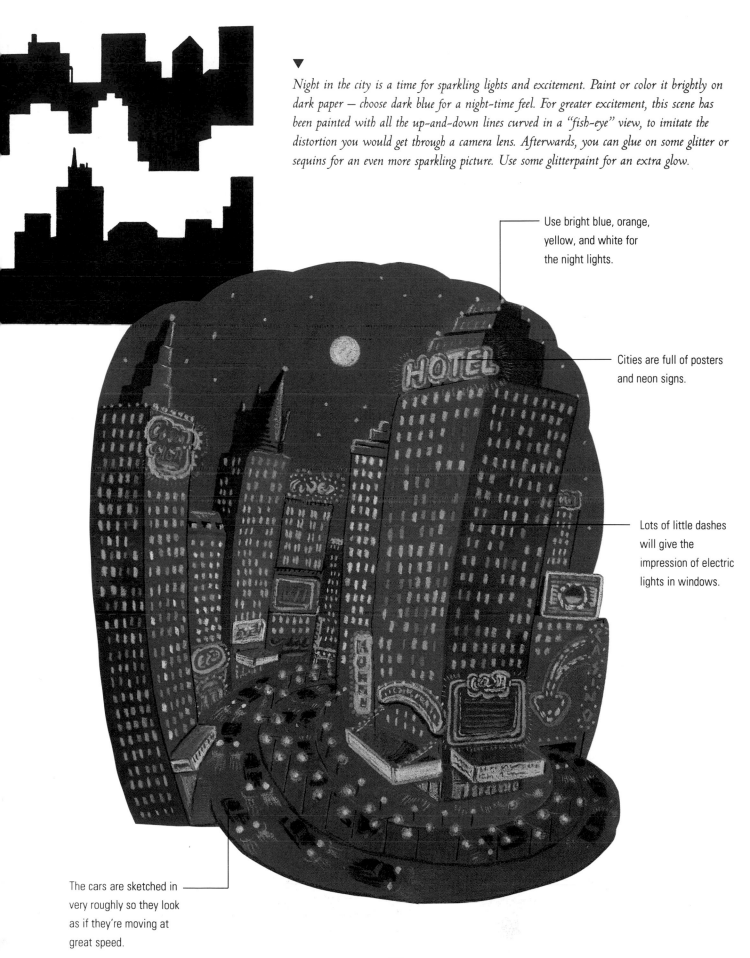

Night in the city is a time for sparkling lights and excitement. Paint or color it brightly on dark paper — choose dark blue for a night-time feel. For greater excitement, this scene has been painted with all the up-and-down lines curved in a "fish-eye" view, to imitate the distortion you would get through a camera lens. Afterwards, you can glue on some glitter or sequins for an even more sparkling picture. Use some glitterpaint for an extra glow.

Use bright blue, orange, yellow, and white for the night lights.

Cities are full of posters and neon signs.

Lots of little dashes will give the impression of electric lights in windows.

The cars are sketched in very roughly so they look as if they're moving at great speed.

59

Painting the sky

YOU CAN USE SKY TO CREATE a mood in a picture. For instance, it could be calm, clear and sunny, or dark and threatening. Skies can form a very important part of outdoor painting. Start by planning out your picture and then painting in at least some of the sky first. That way you can get the right mood before you go on to details and, if you're not happy with your sky, you can start again with a different idea!

▲
Start with broad strokes of strong watercolor blue. Gradually add more white as you get nearer the land.

CLEAR SKIES

For a clear sky, paint in horizontal lines with a thick brush. Start at the top and work downwards, gradually changing color as you go down. The sky should look palest on the horizon line.

▲
Skies aren't always blue! Try an evening sky with threatening gray clouds and a pink sunset.

PAINTING A VAN GOGH SKY

The painter Van Gogh lived in the nineteenth century. He had a unique way of painting, using very small brush strokes in many different closely related colors. These give a wonderful feeling of movement, with swirls and dots of thick bright paint.

It is an extremely effective method for doing skies, as you can see from this picture of his called "The Starry Night." All the stars have such big glows they look like huge planets. Here we give you some tips so that you can try the idea for yourself.

MAKING CLOUDS

Clouds come in lots of different colors, shapes, and sizes. Here are some ideas for basic shapes, using a range of techniques.

▲

Try painting or crayoning on white paper, leaving spaces in the shape of clouds.

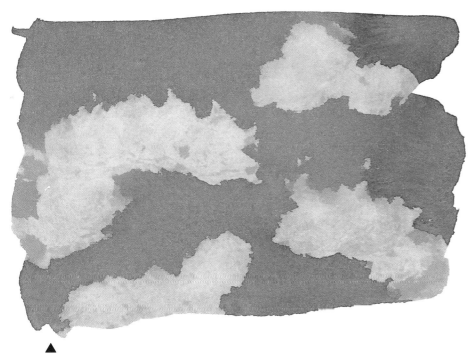

▲

Paint a blue sky with runny poster or watercolor paint. While it's still wet, dab on a soft rag or dry brush to remove patches of paint to make cloud shapes.

▲

Start with an even blue background and paint on fluffy white clouds. Then add gray to the undersides of the clouds to make them look rainy.

Use small, even brush strokes.

Put bright colors on top of a pale background.

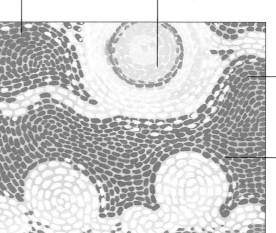

Swirl paint around the sun.

Keep the paint thick.

Winter weather

Getting dramatic weather effects in your paintings can be great fun. Rain, wind, fog and snow can be just as exciting to paint as bright, sunny days. You can use a range of techniques, such as smudgy charcoal, chalks and pastels, and watercolors.
Colored paper is a good choice for dramatic effects. Remember to use shading to give your paintings form, even if your scene has no direct sunlight.

Rain

You don't need to draw in every raindrop. Just suggest rain falling by drawing slanted lines on the top of a scene.

Draw rain lines with charcoal on top of a painted background.

Smudge the lines with your finger or a rag.

Fog and mist

Aim to convey the idea that you can only dimly make things out. Don't put in too much detail, but concentrate on shapes.

Rub lightly over a painting with the side of a piece of white chalk. This creates an effect of rolling mist.

Fill in the basic shapes. Keep thin lines very pale, so that they look indistinct.

Sponge or paint pale gray and white paint all over the sheet to form the background.

Make foreground objects stronger and darker than those in the background.

WIND

You can't see wind, but you can work out which direction it is blowing in by showing what it does to things such as trees, flags, hats, and people's clothes. Make sure that everything in your picture is being blown in the same direction.

Give the kite a dancing tail.

Make sure all the trees lean the same way.

The girl's skirt and hair must blow the same way as the trees.

Make strong blue shadows to show a sunny day in winter. They must all go the same way.

Use white chalk to make snow on colored paper. Show other details in different colored chalks.

SNOW

If you use white paper, you can paint in only the objects, and leave areas unpainted for the snow. Shadows will make the snow look deep — paint them in shades of blue.

Use an old toothbrush to spatter white paint to make a snowstorm.

63

Ways with water

WATER CAN LOOK VERY DIFFERENT depending on the time of day, the light, and the weather. Some water moves fast with lots of ripples or waves. If it is in a stream with lots of pebbles and stones, it will break up into different channels, with swirls and white froth. Some water is calm and still with different-colored reflections on the surface.

Water always reflects what is above it. Remember to put some of the surrounding colors into it, especially the color of the sky.

DRAWING WATER WITH A PENCIL

Don't think you need colors to portray water! Careful pencil shading can suggest many different kinds of water. If you leave areas of the paper white, they will act as highlights to help give a feeling of depth or movement.

Vertical lines show a deep waterfall, with crosshatching at the bottom to show a cloud of spray.

Fine shading and white areas show a large expanse of calm water.

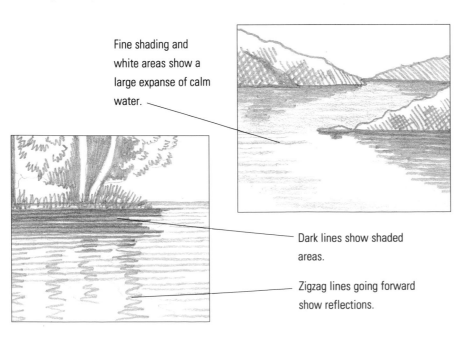

Dark lines show shaded areas.

Zigzag lines going forward show reflections.

Crosshatching in little flicks shows rough water.

PAINTING REFLECTIONS

The way you paint reflections will show what kind of water is in your picture. It could be full of movement, or very calm and still.

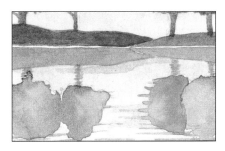

2 When there is a little movement in the water, reflections will be ripply, and colors lighter than the object itself.

3 These reflections are even more broken up, with a little white in them to show the way the light catches the ripples.

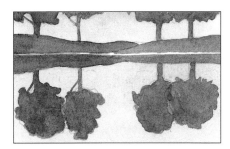

1 In completely calm water, objects are reflected almost perfectly, upside down. The colors are the same, too.

4 Putting in a white zigzag line stretching off to the horizon gives the idea of a reflection from the sun — even if you can't actually see the sun itself.

1 Paint a background of one color for the sea, up to the horizon line. Add a paler wash for the sky, and a sailing boat if you like.

2 Gradually add short strokes of other colors, to represent ripples and broken-up reflections. Long, straight strokes will suggest calm water.

SEA PICTURE

If you build up your picture gradually, you can get just the effect of movement you want in the water. First you should decide where your horizon line is going to be.

Making waves

THE SEA IS ALWAYS MOVING, EVEN on the calmest day. You need to add waves or ripples to show how the light is caught and reflected off the water. If you draw a shoreline, the ripples or waves should follow the same shape. Stormy seas are full of crashing waves and spray. Calm seas will have clear reflections of boats and the sky.

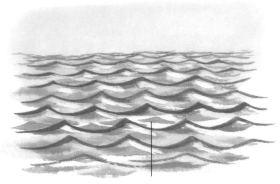

Wave shapes with crests touched in with white show lots of little ripples. Make sure all the waves go the same way.

SEA SHAPES

There are lots of shapes of lines you can make for waves, to convey different kinds of seas and weathers. Practice them using all your different pencils, crayons, and paints.

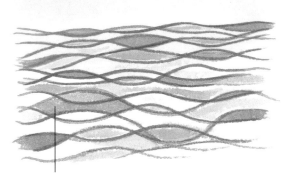

Wavy lines filled in with blues and greens create a more abstract idea of the sea.

Lots of little dashes in blue and green ink suggest a lively, constantly moving sea.

Broad strokes made with chalk pressed down on its side give the idea of a calm, almost waveless, sea.

ROUGH SEAS

To make a storm picture, try using charcoal and chalk smudged together, or thick paint dragged into wave shapes with the edge of a piece of cardboard.

1 First put on your background with even watercolor paints. Then put on a few blobs of different, sea colors. The blobs must be of thick paint, not too runny.

2 Using the edge of a piece of card, drag the blobs in curves to make wave shapes. The colors will all mix together.

3 When the sea colors are dry, paint the tips of the waves with white, and splatter on more white with a toothrush to make sea spray.

SUNSET SEAS

At sunset, the water reflects the red and orange colors of the sun, in a broad band at the front and getting narrower towards the vanishing point on the horizon. You can put in these reflections even if the sun has disappeared from the picture.

Use white and paler shades of the sky colors for the setting sun's reflection in the water.

Foreground objects, like the shoreline, the trees, and the boat, will appear in silhouette against the brightness of the sun's glow.

Flowers

Flowers have inspired outdoor painters for many hundreds of years. You can paint or draw them realistically or use them to make imaginative abstract designs. They can be painted in delicate watercolors or bold, bright poster paint. Start by looking carefully at their different shapes and colors.

▲

If you put different watercolors together while wet, they will run together and smudge slightly, giving a very delicate effect.

BASIC FLOWER SHAPES

Some flowers grow in simple shapes, and others are very complicated. Whichever they are, it helps to start with simplified shapes when you draw them. Look at all the flowers you can find and see how many fit into these shapes. Make sketches of other shapes for yourself.

Roses are shaped like bowls.

Daisy-style flowers are round like a plate.

Some flowers have long fine stalks called stamens that come out from the center. These have rounded tips.

Lily-style flowers are shaped like trumpets.

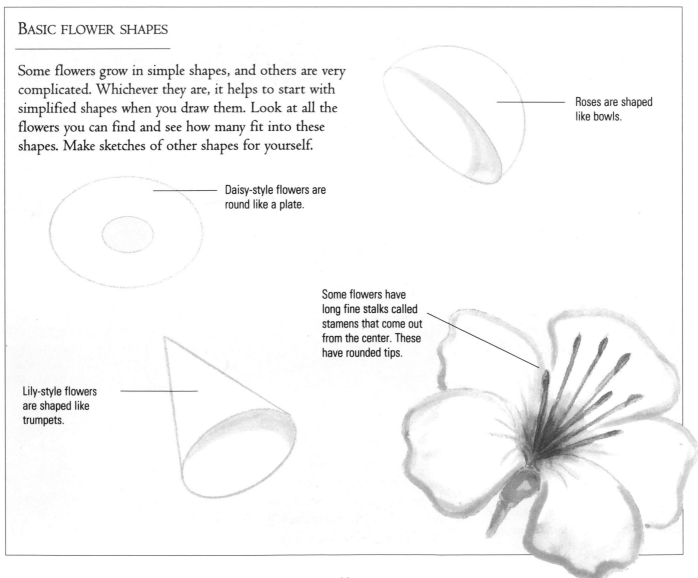

FLOWERS IN THE LANDSCAPE

You can position flowers in outdoor paintings to help you create different points of view. Remember the rules of perspective – things look bigger the nearer they are.

▲

This is a view from the middle distance, with the flowers mostly the same size, but relatively much bigger then the trees.

▲

Here is a view from much nearer the ground. Because the flowers are much closer, see how they are bigger and more detailed.

▲

This view is from high up on a hill. The flowers are so tiny that they are just dots of different color, without any detail.

FLOWERS STEP BY STEP

Start with a fine pencil outline.

If you want to paint a flower realistically, it is best to build it up gradually. This daisy is done using poster paint.

Put fine shading around the top petals to separate them from the layer below.

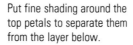

Add detail to the center, the leaves, and the outside edges.

Use big brushes and thick, brightly colored paint. Let each layer of paint dry before you put on the next.

Make sure that the shaded parts – of the bowl and the leaves – are all on the same side, and that the light casts a shadow.

FLOWERS IN STRONG LIGHTING

If you paint flowers against a very dark background with bright colors, they will really glow. This is a different approach from the daisy. It doesn't try for realistic detail, but gets the effect by the right shapes and colors, and realistic shadows and highlights.

More flower ideas

ONCE YOU HAVE MASTERED THE basic shapes and colors of flowers, and practiced different painting techniques, you can go on to more adventurous things. Here we show you how to make flower "paintings" out of paper, and how to paint in oriental and abstract styles.

FLOWERS FROM PAPER

These beautiful flowers are very easy to make with pieces of colored paper. First sketch out your flower shapes and plan what colors to use. Then cut out the different shapes. When you have successfully copied these, try making up your own!

◀

Cut out your shapes from each piece of colored paper. Glue the big pieces at the front together first, then add the separate leaves and petals to the back.

FIELDS OF FLOWERS

Flowers can either be close up, and shown in detail, or part of a bigger landscape. Look at the poppies in the picture on the left, by the French Impressionist Claude Monet (for more about the Impressionists, see page 33). The ones in the foreground are made of two shades of red, to show light and shade. Further back, they are just one color. The artist has made them look just like poppies, but without painting any detail such as stems.

ORIENTAL FLOWERS

In China and Japan artists use pale, washy watercolors or inks to make very delicate, simple pictures of flowers and trees. Much of the paper is often left unpainted. You can get a similar effect by using cream or white watercolor paper.

Occasionally add stronger colors or black to give the picture variety.

Use dots of different sizes and colors on top of a green field to show meadow flowers.

Use mostly delicate colors like gray and pale green. Keep the paint thin and watery, and the shapes very simple, with short brush strokes.

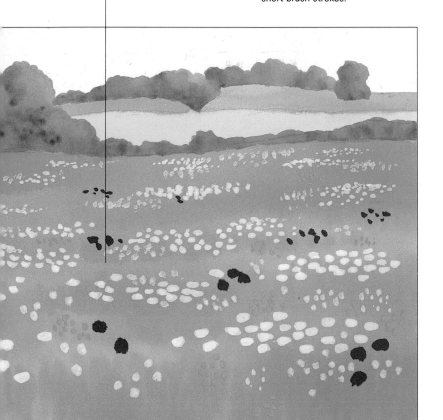

FLOWER PATTERNS

Flower shapes and colors make good abstract patterns. If you want to do stripes, start with fine ruled pencil marks to help you keep them straight. You won't be able to see the pencil marks when you have finished painting.

Trees

No TWO TREES ARE THE SAME. They grow in all kinds of shapes and sizes. Their colors change with the seasons, the time of day, the weather, and the light of the sun or moon.

Sometimes they look dark and threatening; sometimes they look bright and colorful. They make an ideal subject for painting or drawing at any time of the year.

▲

Leaves in the Fall are among the most beautiful and colorful things you'll ever want to paint. See how patterns are made in these maple leaves in different colors that follow the shape of the veins. Try copying part of this photograph using your paints - mix the colors

WHAT TO LOOK AT

Start by looking at lots of different trees and outlining their general shapes, both the trunk and the branches. Here are some common shapes — see if you can find others.

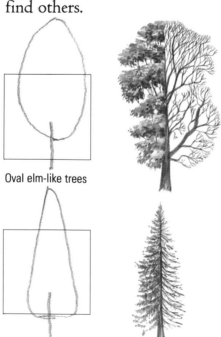

Oval elm-like trees

Tall fir-like trees

Tall, thin poplar-like trees

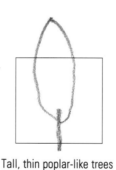

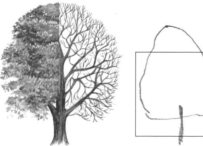

Bushy oak-like trees

LEAVES

Leaves are not only different shapes and sizes, but very different colors. They range from golden to bluey greens and in the Fall they can be glorious reds, yellows, and browns. Look carefully at the shapes, and see which shape belongs to which tree.

Heart-shaped leaves

Finger-like leaves

Elongated leaves

Feather-like leaves

PAINTING A TREE IN STAGES

One of the best ways to paint trees is to build up the paint gradually. Choose your colors and sketch your outline first. If you want your tree to look realistic, make sure its shape, leaf shape and color all match up. You can either look at the trees around you, or check picture books for more ideas.

Outline the tree's shape with watery paint and a thin brush. Then paint in some shaded areas of foliage, and strengthen the color of the trunk. Paint in the sky around the tree and in any gaps between the branches. When the paint is dry, finish off by adding more light and dark to show the effects of the light on the leaves.

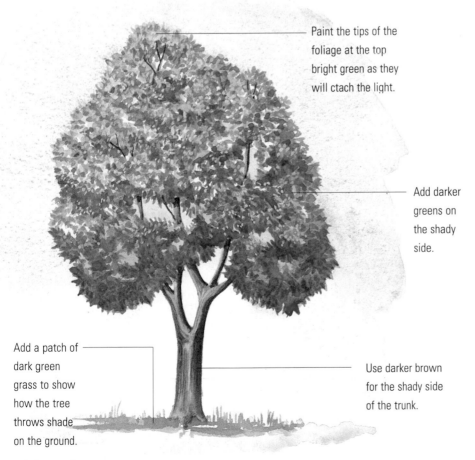

Paint the tips of the foliage at the top bright green as they will ctach the light.

Add darker greens on the shady side.

Add a patch of dark green grass to show how the tree throws shade on the ground.

Use darker brown for the shady side of the trunk.

USING TREES TO SHOW DISTANCE

When you are painting or drawing a landscape you can use trees to help you create a sense of depth. If you are painting a wood, overlap the trees slightly, and shade each one differently. Make the trees in the front bigger than those further away.

TACKLING TREE TRUNKS

Look at the trunks of trees as well as their foliage. Bark can be really interesting to draw and paint. See what kind of patterns and colors it has, and use paints or crayons to practice drawing different kinds.

Special tree effects

LOOK AT TREES AT DIFFERENT times of the day and the year, and see how varied they are. Deciduous trees lose their leaves in winter, when you can see their shape in the branches. Evergreens keep their leaves, but the color changes. The leaves aren't the only important part! Think about blossoms and fruits as well.

SPONGING LEAVES

You can make a tree look convincing without painting leaves in great detail. Paint two colors for the foliage. While they are still wet, blot off excess paint with kitchen paper or tissue. This will mix the colors together.

When the greens are dry, dab on darker colors with a sponge

TREES FOR ALL SEASONS

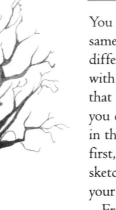

You can have fun painting the same tree as it appears at different times of year. Start with the winter view of a tree that loses its leaves, so that you can see the shape clearly in the branches. Sketch this first, and you can copy the sketch as the first step for all your other ones.

Fruit trees will have pretty blossom in spring, thick green leaves in the summer, and bright fruits in the Fall. Or you can paint a tree like a maple, which has beautiful glowing colors in the Fall.

SPIKY SHAPES WITH A STRAW

One way to make different colors blend together well is to blow paint through a straw. This makes the paint go off in different directions into exciting shapes. For trees, choose different greens, browns, and yellows that go together well. If you want all the colors to stay separate, let each one dry before you do the next; if you want them to mix together, work with them wet. You can use this technique for lots of different subjects.

1 Start with watery paint and put a blob on the page with your brush. Then blow on to the paint through a straw (not too hard!) to make it spread.

2 Add different colors, one by one, and repeat the straw blowing. When the blotches have all dried, you can add more details with a dryish brush.

DEAD TREES

Dead trees are spiky and jagged. Try drawing them with a soft black pencil or smudgy charcoal on white paper. For a dramatic, more abstract effect, you can also try using white or pale colored chalks on dark paper.

A TREE SILHOUETTE

Draw or paint around the outline of a tree, leaving the white space for the tree itself. Plan the outline and draw it carefully in pencil before you start. Use a bright, strong color so that the tree shape will stand out.

75

Think BIG!

WHY NOT TRY A HUGE painting? You can put it on your wall so that it looks like a mural - or even paint a mural directly on the wall if you're allowed! The trick with really big paintings is to plan them first small, using an ordinary sheet of drawing paper. Then you "scale them up," which means transferring the plan to the final size.

▼

Decide on a unit of measurement - say, two inches - and mark the measurements carefully on all four sides of your painting or tracing paper overlay. Then join the marks together with a ruler, to make two-inch squares all over.

SCALING

First sketch out your painting in pencil in the usual way. It's a good idea at this stage to paint a small version, too. This is because it is much easier to decide on the colors and the composition at a small scale. Also, it doesn't matter too much if you make a mistake!

When you have completed the small version and the paint has dried, rule a squared grid on the painting. If you prefer, you can use a separate piece of tracing paper for the grid, and lay it over the painting, taping them together so the grid doesn't slip. This means you do not spoil the small painting, and you can re-use the grid for another project.

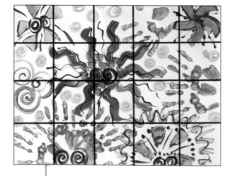

Use a ruler to join
your marks so that the
grid is straight.

▲

Use wallpaper lining for big sheets of paper, and join several widths together if you need to. Draw a grid very lightly on it in pencil, with the same number of squares, but much bigger than the original squares, depending on how big you want your final painting to be. Copy your painting carefully, square by square, in a rough pencil sketch. When you are satisfied, put on the color, referring to your small version for help.

BIG PAINTING IDEAS

Here are examples of big paintings and murals done outside. See how the composition should be kept fairly simple when you are painting on a large scale. You'll need spray-paints, or very big brushes, such as wallpaper and decorating brushes. Or have fun smearing the paint on using your fingers and hands.

◀ *The spray-paint colors in this mural really glow, and the texture of the wall is a valuable part of the painting.*

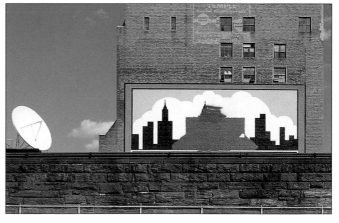

◀ ▲ *In the mural of the boy dancing on the piano keys, the supports of the outside wall have been used as a part of the composition. In the city silhouette, the simple, strong shapes show up well on the blank wall beneath the windows - keeping to only three colors plus black has added to the effect.*

77

Painting on glass

GLASS IS AN EXCELLENT THING TO paint on, since the light shines through it, making the colors glow. You've probably seen pictures on clear plastic for hanging in front of your window - they're often made to look like stained-glass windows. Here we show you how to make your own!

To make a background color, glue a whole sheet of tissue paper over the acetate, and paint it. Then continue with your collage. The light will shine through the background color, making it look very bright.

▲

Use different colored tissue papers and cut them out to make a collage painting. Glue them carefully on to acetate to make a bright, glowing picture.

PRETEND GLASS PAINTING!

In case you don't have a window you're allowed to paint on, you can get the same result by using clear plastic. You can buy this in stationers and art supplies shops - it is called acetate and is not very expensive.

If you arrange the tissue paper so that it makes layers, you can create deeper lines of color which act as shading.

PAINTING ON GLASS

To paint directly on to a window, use thick poster paint. Mix the paint with some dishwashing liquid instead of water - this makes it easy to wipe off again. You may get drips: wipe them off quickly with a damp rag, and paint over the gap again. If you use "glow in the dark" paints, you can even enjoy your painting at night!

▲

These exotic birds were painted with thick paints, in layers of color. Let each layer dry before you add the next. Finally, add some sparkly gold or silver. You will get a different

▼

Paint an exotic beach scene on your window to cheer yourself up in winter! Look at pages 44-45 for tips on how to do the sea by dragging thick paint with a comb. You can also use the end of your paintbrush to scratch lines out of the

79

Textured rubbings

Y OU'VE PROBABLY HEARD OF BRASS rubbing, when you lay a piece of paper over an engraved brass and rub all over it with a crayon to make the pattern come through. You can do exactly the same with textured objects such as leaves, tree bark, bricks, and stones. Use wax crayons, chalks, and charcoal, and experiment with colored papers. Cut out your rubbings and make them into collages.

Charcoal gives a
dark, smoky effect.

EXPERIMENTAL TEXTURES

Use medium thickness paper to make rubbings of leaves. If the pattern doesn't come through very well, try thinner paper. Don't use really thin paper, because it might tear. Try charcoal, and different-colored wax crayons.

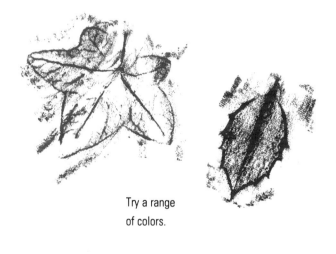

Try a range
of colors.

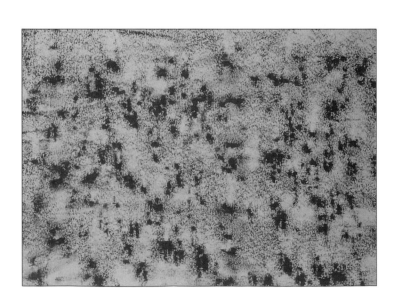

▲ ▶ *These rubbings were made using rough-textured pieces of tree bark and colored chalks.*

COLLAGE RUBBINGS

Make lots of different rubbings in bright colors and paste them on colored paper to make a collage. You don't have to aim for a realistic arrangement if you don't want to — you can make exciting abstract pictures.

◄

This arrangement of rubbings makes a pretty pattern against the red background. Always plan how you are going to combine colors before you start.

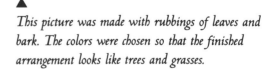

▲

This picture was made with rubbings of leaves and bark. The colors were chosen so that the finished arrangement looks like trees and grasses.

◄

Here is a lovely tree which stands out against the dark background. It is fun to make rubbings that match up with what you are going to create in your collage. Here, leaf rubbings make the leaves, and a bark rubbing the trunk.

81

Ancient art

FOR THOUSANDS OF YEARS people have painted scenes of the outdoors. Many ancient civilizations thought that the landscape and animals around them had magical powers. They painted what they saw in order to collect some of the magic. You can easily paint in some of the same ways, like dabbing and splattering.

▲ Pictures of hands made by Native Americans on a rock in New Mexico.

MAKING YOUR OWN HAND PRINT

Hands have been used as a decoration and a subject for painting since ancient times. Here we show you how to make a print in the old way. If you do this on your own, you will only be able to make one hand print at a time. It's more fun to get a friend to help you, and take it in turns to make prints of both your hands.

1 Lay the paper flat, and put one hand firmly on the center, palm down, with the fingers spread out.

2 Shake the powder all round your hand, making sure it goes between your fingers.

3 Lift your hand off quickly and cleanly. There'll be powder on it, so take care not to let it fall on to your print.

4 If you want to keep the print, fix the powder firmly in place by spraying the paper all over evenly with aerosol fixer.

▲ On the left we show you how to make a hand print exactly the same way as this one, painted many years ago in a cave in Australia. For this, the artist probably made a pale powder from soft stone, to show up against the brown surface.

WHAT YOU NEED
....
Black powder paint
Coarse sugar paper
Spray fixer

STONE AGE STYLE PAINTING

Stone Age people lived over 20,000 years ago. They painted pictures on cave walls, showing animals that they hunted. They made their paints from different colored earth and pieces of burnt wood, getting brown, yellow, orange, red, and black. The picture on the left shows a deer from a cave at Altamira, Spain. You can easily recreate Stone Age painting by following these simple steps.

1 Paint a cream background. Use cotton wool to lightly dab on some patches of reddy-brown and grey. When the paint is dry rub it over lightly with fine sandpaper to make it look like stone.

2 Draw a simple animal shape in charcoal or black wax. Fill it in with cotton-wool dabs of reddy-brown. When the paint dries, sandpaper the painting to make it look patchy and old.

NATIVE AMERICAN PAINTING

Native Americans used painting to tell stories of their outdoor adventures. Their colors were made from plants and earth, but you can get a similar effect by using watercolor pencils or paint. The artists often used symbols for objects, based on simple abstract drawings of them. We've shown some for hailstones, lightning, mountains, and rainbows. Try copying them to make your own Native American painting.

Lightning

Hailstones

Mountains

Buffalo

Rainbow

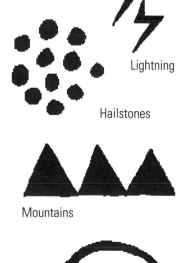

Colorful collages

Y OU CAN BE VERY INVENTIVE MAKING
pictures from all kinds of unusual materials.
As well as paper and fabric - which are great for
different colors and textures - collect objects from
where you live or from holidays in the country or
at the beach.

THE MATERIAL WORLD

Fabric gives a wonderful range of
colors and textures for an outdoor
picture. Plan your picture first,
then choose the right colors for
each part of it. Aim for
appropriate textures, too - e.g.
soft green fabric for the hills
which you can fold.

<table>
<tr><td colspan="2">WHAT YOU NEED</td></tr>
<tr><td colspan="2" align="center">Glue</td></tr>
<tr><td colspan="2" align="center">Stiff card</td></tr>
<tr><td colspan="2" align="center">Large fabric pieces
for background</td></tr>
<tr><td colspan="2" align="center">Smaller fabric scraps for objects</td></tr>
</table>

These clouds are made from scraps of white lace.

You can buy ready-made fabric flowers at department stores. Or make your own!

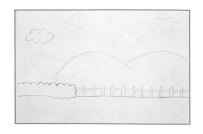

I *Start by sketching your picture in soft pencil. Use stiff card or thick paper so that it won't tear when you glue things to it.*

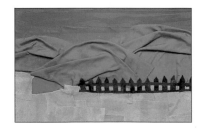

2 *Cut out the large background pieces of fabric. Glue them on to the card. Make folds in the green fabric for the hills.*

3 *If you like, paint shading on top of the fabric to help give a sense of depth. Use watery paint so that you don't hide the original color.*

▲

When you have sketched out your picture and glued everything in place, you can add great depth and atmosphere by painting varnish all over it so that it shines. This is especially good on a dark background color.

PAPER ART

This colorful outdoor picture was made from scraps of different papers. Use tissue paper, old newspapers (you can paint or crayon colors on them), and clothes cut out of magazines.

TRASH ART

A space picture makes a great choice for using a kinds of shiny objects. Try sequins and glittery beads on a thread, pins and safety pins, old metal fasteners, bits of zipper, nails and screws, nuts and bolts - the list is endless!

Working with photographs

YOUR CAMERA IS A VERY USEFUL ACCESSORY for painting the outdoors. It's much quicker to take a snapshot than paint a picture! So take shots to help you later, with things like lighting effects, the positions of shadows, and perspective. You can also use your favorite shots as part of your paintings. You can paint fantasy backgrounds for familiar things or people, and make collages out of photographs you have taken yourself or cut out of magazines.

PHOTO PICTURES

Why not make an exotic background for your own home? This would make an amusing greetings card to send to your friends! Cut out your home from a photograph, then sketch out the background you want to paint. Trace in the outline of the building and paint a bit inside the outline so that no edges will show. Then glue the photograph in the space.

▲

Put your friends and family in some unexpected places! Paint the mountain scene first, then glue the figures on top of it. To add realism, put in shadows so that the people really look part of the scene.

PHOTO COLLAGES

Lots of famous artists have made collages out of different photographs taken from papers and magazines. You can do the same, putting in some photos of your own if you like. Use thick paper or card that won't tear when glued, and try different background colors. Like any painting, plan it first, thinking about colors and composition. Then just lay the photographs in place to have a final check before you paste them down.

◄

Collages can be made from all sorts of things — this one like the picture below has come from torn up magazines.

▼

This collage was made with background papers of plain color or slightly patterned, with details such as the house and the tiled pot of flowers taken from magazines. The birds were drawn afterwards with black pen.

87

Still life collages

TWIGS, FLOWERS, LEAVES, AND BARK ARE USUALLY easy to collect. Look out for seashells, too, and other things from the beach. You can even use dried things from the kitchen, such as pasta shapes, pulses, and beans. Combine your "found objects" with painting for a varied and original effect.

FLOWER PICTURES

Plan a flower painting using real flowers, stems, bits of bark, and twigs. Ordinary flowers that have died can look very striking, but for the longest-lasting result use pressed, dried flowers in bright colors.

1 Sketch your outlines first on a spare piece of paper. This makes a guide for you to copy so that you'll have no pencil marks on the finished picture.

2 Glue all your collected bits on to stiff card or thick paper, using your sketch as a guide. See how the twigs can be arranged to give different effects.

3 Add a painted background in watery paint and, if you like, some painted flowers as well. Painting some of the twigs gold will really make the picture glow.

Dried pasta, grains, beans, and pulses make wonderfully colorful pictures – and they don't cost much! Use a combination of colored pasta, and shapes that you paint yourself, especially gold and silver.

This one is very easy! Simply collect lots of different shells from the beach and paint a sea background of high waves. If you like, add sand as well. Make shapes on the paper in glue, and sprinkle sand on before the glue dries. You can collect different colored sand from some beaches.

If you collect fir branches, fir cones and twigs, you can make a whole forest scene. Arrange the twigs in the shape of fir trees, and design a forest floor of fallen twigs and cones. Choose deep blue card for a night sky and add silver stars. Glittery gold and silver paint will make the scene look moonlit.

Maps and models

A MAP IS A REPRESENTATION OF A place with symbols for features such as roads, rivers, and buildings.

Professional ones are made for helping you find your way around, but maps can also be very beautiful, just like paintings. Here we give you ideas for flat maps, and also for 3D maps, which are more like models.

A FLAT MAP

Try making a flat map of the area near your home. Take some measurements, so that you get things the right distance apart - this is called "scale." It's easier to get the scale right if you use squared paper - ten squares, for example, could represent one mile. Use an existing map to help you if you need to.

▲ *Sketch your map first lightly in pencil so that you can correct any mistakes. Design symbols for all the different things you will be showing - there are tips on the right. Color in the symbols with your paints.*

KEY TO MAP SYMBOLS

The key can be on the same sheet as the map, or separate. Use your neatest handwriting for the labels.

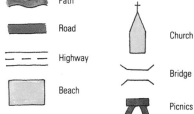

Pool

Path

Road

Highway

Beach

Games pitch

Sea

Shop

View

Roundabout

Mountain

House

Church

Bridge

Picnics

Forest

Railroad

Park

River

Camping

Making a 3D map

A 3D map works the same way as a flat one, but you can have fun making models to represent things, instead of drawing symbols. Use sugar paper or thin card to make these in different colors.

1 First sketch out your map in pencil on a sheet of paper as a guide. This one is drawn at an angle, so the buildings all look solid. Put in the features you want to show.

2 Use stiff paper such as sugar paper, or thin card to make your models. Make sure each model is in scale – the tree here is a bit taller than the building.

3 On a big piece of stiff paper, arrange the flat elements in the composition. We have shown two roads crossing each other, a river, the shoreline and a park.

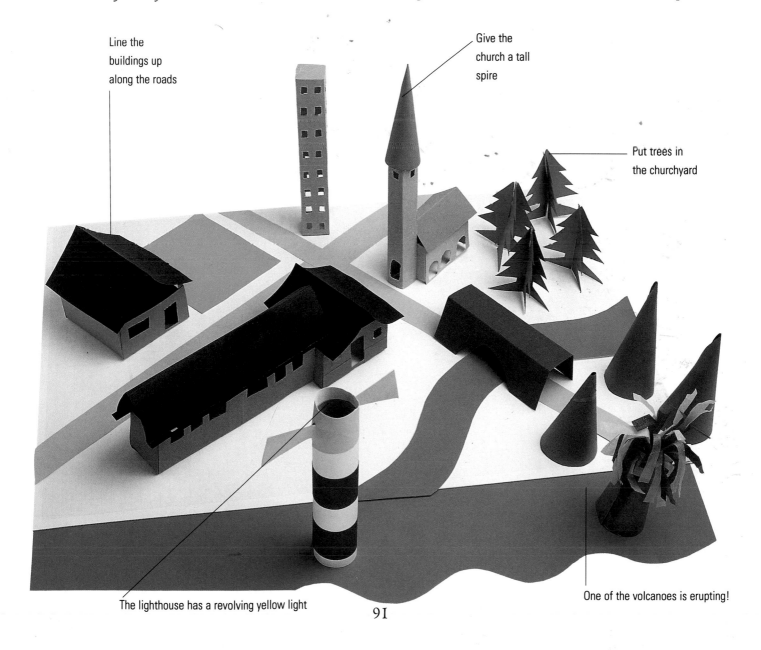

Line the buildings up along the roads

Give the church a tall spire

Put trees in the churchyard

The lighthouse has a revolving yellow light

One of the volcanoes is erupting!

Index